Answer the Door

Christopher Bursk

FUTURECYCLE PRESS
www.futurecycle.org

Cover artwork, "Before It Begins" by Justin Bursk; cover and interior book design by Diane Kistner; Caecilia text and titling

Library of Congress Control Number: 2020931328

Published by FutureCycle Press
Athens, GA 30607

ISBN 978-1-942371-89-2

For Ethel Rackin, Jim Fillman, Joanne Leva, Carolina Morales,
and Wendy Fulton Steginsky
who watch over a language we cannot live without

For Barbara Simmons and Steve Nolan
who watch over this fragile world

&

For Mary Ann
who watches over me

☩

*But were my heart to stop from breaking
I would have loved in vain;
had my heart ceased its aching
for others' uncooled pain
I would have lived in vain.*

Bernadette McBride: *Conversation with Emily*

Contents

Confiscated Weapons

Which story do you want? Ed Z. asks.
The one I tell the lawyers or the one nobody wants
to hear?
            In high school
I had no inkling I'd end up behind bars
listening to a young man read a sonnet
about cutting his father from the rafters.
He didn't know what to do with the knife
afterwards. Throw it away?
                        Keep it? Use it again?
In Ricky Dee's villanelle he keeps shouting
at his mother on the floor,
as if she's not dead, just obstinate.
Everyone in jail has a secret he wants
pried from him, a grief she's doing her best
to make sense of, account books full of the wrongs
done to us:
            Nick's competing versions
of what happened the night he killed his brother;
Steven's ingenious fabrication
of why he was ambushed in the library
with his arm in a child's pants;
Tiny's quiet misery; Frannie's principled rage;
Mary Ellen's missing trash bag
of cocaine.
            As a boy I was too busy
hurting myself to suspect
how much hurt there was in the world.
                    Now every week
it's reunion time in prison:
One man cries when he speaks of his daughter.
Another looks down at his hands
as if he can't believe all they've done.
                        We swap stories,
each of us hoping for a lighter sentence
than we know we deserve.

1

*The sunlight made young Christopher's red hair seem on fire.
"One night on the water," his father told him, "And you'll be glad
you're a weaver's son."*

Meet Christopher Columbus by Jan deKay
Illustrated by John Edens

Rafe

Here is the latest list of boys
I've decided not to kill: Bobby Davenport,
Paul Miglacci, Denny Clifford, Richie Webb,
Nick Winter, Eddie Schacht.
One night I went to bed, an ordinary kid,
and the next morning I knew
if I touched a classmate in a certain way
he'd die; and because I am not sure
exactly which way I could hurt him
—only that I could—I'm careful not to
brush against anyone, all day,
all week. *How was school?* my mother asks
in a way that makes it clear
she's not really interested in an answer.
Every day she turns herself smaller and smaller
till she's a fine powder
anyone could scatter to the wind
only to have it blow back in his face.
What are you doing? my teacher demands.
Even after she seizes my pencil
I keep drawing.
Maybe someday I'll come back
to this school and shoot her.
Probably I won't. After all,
it's not been that bad a day,
even if I've been punched in the face
by Dickie Ainslie and sent to the principal for refusing
to say who bloodied my nose.
As soon as I shut my bedroom door,
I pull off my clothes
and dive into the closet
and spend the rest of the afternoon in its quarry
of darkness, its secret pools.
I swim till too tired to do anything
but sleep. Rafe,
the boy I've invented for occasions like this,
kisses me on the brow the way a father might,
for no reason at all.
Maybe it'll be a good day tomorrow too.

Answer the Door

There was an unpeeled orange
on the kitchen table
and a knife
plunged into the week-old fruit
as if someone had intended
not to eat the orange
but punish it.
Men knocked at the door.

There was a mother
just inside the front door
sitting up straight the way children do
when told not to
move. Every day she dressed
to go out, though
she never did. It was bright
outside, but dark
inside. Even the sun
couldn't persuade the door
to open.

Open the door,
the men said with such authority
you have to admire the woman
for not letting them in.

There had been kindness
in the men's voices
at first—as if they were coaxing a cat
out of a tree. But not now.
The men kept knocking.

Just a minute! I'm coming!
the boy shouted, but he did not
get up from the kitchen table.
On the table was an orange
with a knife
plunged into it.

How hard would it be to pull out the blade?

This is the only story the boy knows
to tell. How he wanted
to answer the door. How he didn't.

Recess

Because I keep waiting to be beat up
at recess—it happened
just once, but once was enough to expect it
to happen again—
I take tiny plastic warriors to school,
a pocketful of Vatsongas I've bought off the back
of a comic book. What luck!
For a few dollars I have a small army:
men girded in loincloths, wearing nothing
else but jackal teeth necklaces
and strips of cowhide fastened tight
around their arms.
Any nine-year-old could use a bodyguard
and now I have two dozen,
men who know what it's like
to be attacked when all you want
is to be left alone.

The Names of Matches

After school I hurry home to the matchbooks
I've hoarded. I owe that to the fire
waiting in each match to be freed.
I cup my hand around the orphan flame
as if only I might protect it.
If I can't be sick enough for my father
to stay home or sad enough
for my mother to give up breaking dishes,
at least I can give birth
to as many flames as I wish:
Sometimes one sways back and forth
as if teetering over a great abyss.
Sometimes a flame bows down before me.
Sometimes it stretches out a sword.

Are you lost?

For Jack and for Jonathan

Are you lost?
the man with bags under both arms asks.
He's the size of a peanut
and makes his living
carrying luggage much too heavy for other men.
My brother's train set fills half of the cellar with its rivers
and mountains, its blinking metropolis
and manicured suburbs, its industries, its freight yard.
I don't dare move the trains.

Not even with the tips of my fingers.
I'm one of those boys
who don't always need their hands
to play. I look
and look into store windows, trespass on back porches,
shrink to enter the church,
school, firehouse, city hall,
swing from a lamppost, climb the bell-tower,
walk up to a girl and kiss her,
drape my arm around a boy
as if we've been pals forever,
bum a cigarette off a man,

and doze next to a drunk at the train station.
I make myself fall asleep
and descend into mine shaft
and volcano, tunnels so dark I wake
scared and even smaller
than the commuters on the train platform
with their tiny briefcases and newspapers,
all of them with somewhere important to go.
Have you been separated from your family?
the red-cap asks.
I love every wrinkle on his burnt sienna face,
the way he grins at me
as if it's no shame to be a kid and lost.

Are you okay? Though weighed down
with other people's urgent business,
he takes the time
to ask me that. *Yes,* I say.
Now I am.

King Solomon's Mines

For Siriaque (1922-1964)

My first trip to the Dark Continent I kept my brother
on my left and the movie theater aisle
on my right. Africa had so many rivers,
and at my age all I needed to do was see water
and I was ready to make more of it
even if meant missing Stewart Granger
putting a bullet into yet another alligator's head.
What just happened? I whispered so loud
Deborah Kerr could've heard me.
In Mount Suliman's shadows she had her husband's map
open. *Deeper,* she commanded.
We must go deep,
and so my brother and I pushed into the jungle
with her. She was a diamond, implacable
light to be held only by the fingertips,
but I didn't fall in love with her as much
as with young Prince Umbopa
whose fathers went back all the way to ancient Egypt.
The previews had promised *rogue elephants,*
battles between long boats,
stampedes of too many kinds of animals to count,
snakes capable of swallowing men whole,
and *natives who've never seen a white woman before.*
But I hadn't expected all that furniture
slung over natives' shoulders, steamer trunks
crammed with biscuits and tea,
so much equipment required
to steal a fortune right out from under
the bloodthirsty eyes of savages,
and so many Caucasian bodies in their tents turning dark
with lust oozing out of every pore.
Sometimes a kid's life is changed
by a father leaving or a favorite grandmother dying
but mine was never the same
after King Solomon's mines.
If there was a lesson to that movie
my brother and I sat through twice,

18

maybe it was that every treasure hunt ends in bones
picked clean. Deborah Kerr beat her hands
against Stewart Granger's sweaty chest,
but I didn't care. I'd seen a man wrestle another man
naked, and I danced with natives
so tall and wiry they could've been trees
that had picked up their roots
and gone on safari.
Their bodies were covered with ash
as if they'd survived more than one fire.
And when I looked at my brother,
he too was staring at Prince Umbopa
who had something still to teach us
nothing else in our lives could.
We stayed in the theater long after everyone left.
The son of kings might rise yet again.

What I Wanted Every Christmas

Marauders, outlaws, a pirate crew,
a renegade tribe,

men who know how to kill,
men with quivers and axes

and hooks for hands
with knives between their teeth

or bearing crosses on their shields
or sitting high on armored horses,

a copper-skinned warrior riding bareback,
a conscripted young soldier

wounded so gravely
he didn't flinch when I touched his face.

I knew what he wanted to tell me
before he spoke.

Don't tell me he didn't speak.
I heard every word he said.

The Book of Knowledge, 1926 edition

1

Open to the right page and you can build a house
out of toothpicks, master French,
swim the rivers of South America,
temper a knife blade, run cable under the Atlantic,
or make an arrow fly straight to its mark.
Perhaps today you'll turn your watch into a compass
or sew a parachute from your father's old silk shirts.
Prying open the tomb of a king
who *has slept for over 3,000 years,*
maybe you won't wish you had enough matches
to burn down the house.

2

Guess which page I turned to
in my grandfather's *Book of Knowledge?*
Had he ever been intrigued as I was
by the twenty-five feet of bowels coiled
inside the human body along with *thousands*
of clever little cells that pass food
into the blood? Inspired by fermentation,
I carried on my own scientific experiments
with colored paper inserted
deep into my nether region—
Crimson, Burnt Sienna, Vermillion, Forest Green
all buried inside me. Had my grandfather
or father ever conducted such investigations?
What did I hope to discover?
Shadows gathered inside me?
Secrets to search out,
despite considerable discomfort?
Some things in the world change
at baffling speed; some things stay
the same, and I suspect
the rectum might prove to be one of these.

3

While my mother cries in the attic
and my father paces downstairs,
I choose to do something sensible:
I open the *Book of Knowledge* and dig for diamonds
or wear bones or memorize birds' eggs
in case I ever happen to travel to England
and come upon a nest belonging to crested wren
or lapwing or nightjar.
I master the mechanics of spider webs,
sailors' knots, how to rewire a lamp,
pi to the fifteenth decimal.
The smaller the print,
the more mystery:
Giant Despair feasting on all who wander into Doubting Castle.
The basket that lifted Christopher Wren to the top of St. Paul's.
A sperm whale with fifty teeth in its lower jaw and none in its upper.
So what if much in its twenty volumes proves outdated?
So is the Bible,
and my grandfather's *Book of Knowledge* has fewer murders
and far more flowers.

4

Bebe pleure et fait le mechant,
Baby cries and makes the naughty child.
Baby cries and is tiresome.

Il veut etre le papa.
He wants to be the papa.
He wants to be papa.

Je lui dis qu'il est trop petit.
I tell him that he is too little.
I tell him that he is too little.

Jeannette le console.
Jenny him comforts.
Jenny comforts him.

Nous sommes fatigues de jouer.
We are tired of to play
We are tired of playing

Bebe dit qu'il a faim
Baby says that he has hunger.
Baby says he is hungry.

Nous avons tous faim.
We have all hunger.
We are all hungry.

5
What Makes a Bee Hum?
Two Fighting Clothespins,
What to Do with a Girl's Work Basket,
The Troubled Land Where a Child Was King,
Don Quixote and the Clouds of Dust,
The War Begun in a Rose Garden,
The Microbes That Did More Mischief than the Wolves,
Why Spiders Do Not Get Caught in Their Own Webs,
The Mystery of Gravity.
While my father tries to figure out
how to keep our mother from killing my brother and me,
I lie in bed with Sir Isaac Newton
so close to my face he could be whispering
to me or I to him.

6
What planet are you on now?
the teacher asks when I open my eyes,
and everyone breaks into laughter.
So I close my eyes again
as tight as I can and when I open them
no one is there, not even the teacher,
and I get up from my desk
and walk out of the classroom and out the front door.
I don't know where I am going—
Madre de Dios? Erta Ale? The Moons of Saturn?—
but I go there anyway.

In a Land of Silky Cats

In a land of women who give birth only to daughters,
I was born, a freak of nature: a boy.

In a country of babies who come into this world singing
as if they can't get over how bright it is,

how much room their outstretched arms have,
I knew not to cry.

In a land where each infant is suckled by many mothers,
the milk proving as delectable a surprise

as all that airy space suddenly surrounding them,
I was given away by my mother

to an old woman with milk just enough
to wet my lips. Who could blame a parent

for shuddering at the sight of me?
In a land where babies learn to speak

as soon as they can open their mouths—
at first they converse just with the birds—

I didn't trust my throat, that fathomless cave,
or my tongue, unruly and ravenous appendage.

Our country traced its beginnings back to fire and lava
and that first immaculate birth

when life, admiring the widows who built a city out of the rubble
their warrior husbands had left as their memorial,

decided to give them only daughters
and have done with penises.

Now silky cats climb high in the branches,
not to massacre the birds nested there

but to get closer to their songs.
Ours was a kingdom of houses so white they drifted

like clouds down the street.
Of course, you don't believe,

you who massacred the Great Auks just for being bon vivants,
and erected towers only to see them topple,

you who nailed a man to a tree
like a no trespassing sign

and have trouble now with any story
you didn't make up.

Here where babies swim before they can walk,
I learned to walk before I could swim—

in other words, I learned to fall.
What misfortune to give birth to a clumsy son

in a world where graceful daughters float from the womb
as if merely leaving one tropical island

for another. At least I wasn't killed immediately
when lifted from the womb.

Right from the start I knew my place.
I dozed with the cats. I made a nest in the trees

and ate what the birds left on the branches.
I did what all freaks learn to do,

all castaways: I kept a daily log
I had no hope of anyone reading.

I'd been spared.
Let me tell you, sometimes that's enough.

2

Questions Anyone Might Want an Answer To,
Book of Knowledge, 1932—Volume 6

Why Are Soap Bubbles Round?
Does Light Weigh Anything?
Why Do the Eyes in Some Portraits Seem to Follow Us?
Why Does a Bad Egg Float?
Why Do We Not Grow Up All at Once?
Why Does an Apple Turn Brown If We Bite and Put It Aside?
Why Do We Press Hard on Down Strokes When Writing?
Why Can We Not Walk Straight with Our Eyes Shut?

.

Ransom

Because the roly-poly man holding a bottle of rum
by the neck has no knife between his teeth,
you make the mistake of begging him
for a mercy you know not to expect
from any of the other pirates.
Your shirt and pants are already ripped off
as if you don't deserve clothes.
It's your favorite way to spend an afternoon:
tied to a stake
like a dog who can run only as far
as his chain lets him.

To your credit, you keep trying the way a dog does—
as if finally it'll solve the riddle of leashes,
hurl itself into all that space
waiting for it. Today you exist
for the amusement of men.
They pour rum down your gullet
till you gag and tilt like a top spun into motion.
Then they watch you wobble
to a stop and then start all over again.
You're a mongrel shaved of its fur.
They could slit your throat any minute—
gut you like a pig,
they tell you over and over—
as if it's more fun making a kid piss himself
than actually carving out his eyes.

Do you really imagine anyone will take pity
on a boy stupid enough
to get himself seized by men
who must've thought his fair skin,
those quivering lips, meant he'd fetch a ransom?
I'm worth a fortune,
you tell the men so often
you almost believe it. *I'm worth a fortune*
but only alive.

Une Martyre

The title drew us the way a scab might
invite fingers to worry its edges.
My brother and I respected scars,
the white thread on his arm
where our mother had broken a glass,
the burn marks on my hand
where she'd put out a cigarette to test my loyalty.
Au milieu des flacons, des étoffes lamées
Et des meubles voluptueux.
Des marbres, des tableaux, des robes parfumées
Qui traînent à plis somptueux.

We didn't have to be well-versed in French
to smell the candles just blown out,
sumptuous women inside voluptuous marble halls.
We raided our father's bookshelves
in search of plague or war or broken heart,
any disaster to pass the hours
between when the hired lady left
and our father came home.
We loved paperbacks that had to be cut open,
pages that must be read with a blade.

My brother's Boy Scout knife liberated Paris
and *des robes parfumées.*
Most of our games ended in martyrdom:
Un cadavre sans tête épanche,
comme un fleuve.... Cadavre—
filling the afternoon with its sweet stench—
French so lovely we hoarded it
the way the moon, that old miser, night after night,
counted its gold. At eight and twelve,
the only way to live with tragedy was to imagine
more tragedy, but of our own making.

Le singulier aspect de cette solitude
Et d'un grand portrait langoureux,
Aux yeux provocateurs comme son attitude,
Révèle un amour ténébreux.

You're even crazier than your mother,
our father muttered, home in time
to snatch *Fleurs de Mal* out of his naked sons' hands.
Even flowers could prove *dangeroux et fatal.*

The Pictures I Look at the Day My Mother Is Taken Back to the Hospital—"For Observation," The Book of Knowledge, Volume 4, 844-846.

1

In the first picture a man is marking a tree that must die.
For many years it has grown in a beautiful lane, but now
it must be sold to a man so houses can be built and tables made.

2

As this picture shows, trees are among the loveliest things
in the world, and we have only to go where there are no trees
to know how they add to the glory of the earth. Yet we must cut them
down, for all strength comes from the earth, and man cannot do
without the strength of a tree.

3

It is easier to uproot a tree when the bark has been stripped
at the bottom and the foot of the tree chopped a little.
The loggers dig under the tree, loosening the roots,
and someone climbs and loops a rope around the treetop.
Pulling the rope, the men below have great power and the tree falls.

4

The first thing once a tree has been felled is to remove its roots.
The branches are trimmed and cut off to make bright fires on winter nights.

5

Here we see a thing of beauty made into a thing of use.

It Happened

It happened,
and then everything in your life happened
either before
or after it.

It happened
and, from then on, all you could think
was why it happened
and what you could've done to stop it happening.

You're seduced again
by that tease, the past tense, its wiles,
the way it leaves a door
ajar, even as it slams it shut.

It happened, and though
life proved far from perfect before it happened,
you miss the luxury
of all that time before it happened.

It happened
so unexpectedly, you keep searching for reasons
why you never expected it
to happen.

It happened.
The anonymity of those two perpetrators:
assassin disguised as pronoun,
thug of a verb.

It happened. In a minute
you will think about it again, and it will happen
again. It happened,
and you could do nothing to stop it,

and so it never stops happening.
See, it is happening now.

Time for Beany

You will have to excuse me, gentlemen. It's Time for Beany.
—Albert Einstein

You too wanted to don a hat with a propeller too
and live on a leaky ship
with a man called Uncle Captain.
You didn't have a TV,
but you did develop a habit of going for strolls
precisely at the time Beany came on
so you could take in a whole show, set by set,
just walking down the street.
Families had their televisions in the front room
in 1952. Everyone turned the volume up
as if they hadn't yet got used to sound
traveling all that distance.
Every night at 5 p.m., you voyaged to Shangri-la-di-da,
Close Shave Cave, the Fifth Corner of the World
and tamed albino gorillas
and won more friends
than you'd thought possible:
Mouth Full of Teeth, Tear-a-long Dotted Lion,
Inca-Dinca Doo Bird.
You even talked Mr. Nobody into giving up his plans
for world domination.
You believed in Beany the way you did in Band-Aids;
sometimes you put on a plaster
even when you didn't have a cut.
You don't remember why
your father hated you—he must've:
why else would he refuse to look at you?—
but you do remember the name of Uncle Captain's ship,
the Leakin' Lena,
and how it always seemed about to sink,
and how it never sank.

For Rick

Harry's and Alice's Only Child Has Some Questions for Beulah

Why is he the *only* child of Harry and Alice?

What does his mother do all day if Beulah beats the rugs, cooks a
    roast, washes *and* dries the dishes?

Who's most beautiful—
    the Beulah with a bun in her hair and a gap between her two
front teeth,
    the Beulah with the tiny mouth and big eyes,
    the Beulah with the darkest eyelashes he's ever seen?

It's a new season. Why don't his mother and father realize
    yet a fourth Beulah's in the kitchen baking his birthday cake?

Why does his mother wear pearls to supper?

Why does his mother talk the way she does?
    She must know the next thing she says
    is going to make his father even more tired than the man
already is?

Why is he so lucky? He pulls on pajamas
    which the summer breezes, with Beulah's help, have turned
fragrant again.
    He climbs into the bed Beulah made and dreams of the
breakfast
    Beulah will have waiting for him in the morning.

Which one will win this evening? The wind or the trees? That long-
    standing quarrel.

It's not so bad a life, is it? he asks Beulah. This morning he's got on
    his cowboy boots, even though they don't really fit anymore,
    and he knows the kids at school will point at them and laugh.

Why don't his mother and father sing to themselves the way all
    the Beulahs do? He too wants Sweet Jesus in his arms.

In memory of Louise Beavers, Ethel Waters,
Hattie McDaniel, and Lillian Randolph

Exodus 17:1-10

Because he's tired of waiting for his father
to come home, he hangs on a bough
till it snaps. He likes the sound wood drags out
as it's broken, each cell of the branch divorced
from its parent cell. If you're eleven,
you rarely get to do anything
that final, that irreparable, so he breaks it
even further. Something that skinny has no right to survive
for long. He cracks the branch so hard
his knee still hurts an hour later.
It's one of those days
when he needs to hurt. So he gets out his knife—
what's a boy without a pocket knife?—
and starts shaving off epidermis till there's nothing left
to protect the wood. The blade punishes each layer
it cuts through. Afterwards he's almost embarrassed
to take the stick in his hand,
it's that naked, and that's why
he knows he finally has the right staff
to carry into the woods
to the rock he's been attempting to split open
for weeks. He'd tried the rock before
with a baseball bat, an oar, a crowbar, a shovel,
only to realize he needed something that'd been living
barely minutes before
it struck the rock. He'll make the rock pay
for being so intractable it won't even spark
when hit. He'll be just as pigheaded
as Moses. Break up that claustrophobic stone.
Hammer till it surrenders its spring
of water he'll cup in his palm, lift to his lips.
He isn't thirsty, but still he strikes the rock
and strikes it and strikes it and strikes it
and strikes it and strikes it.

for Duncan

What I Wouldn't Mind Being

Something the frost can't kill
no matter how hard it tries,

a weed so nondescript
no one has thought to name it,

thumbprints for petals,
a flower so smudged who'd think of picking it,

roots so resilient you could pluck up the whole plant
and still it'd blossom in the compost

like a rat living off garbage,
one of those vines you think you've exterminated

but that keeps taking back its small portion
of the yard, too busy being a weed

in a field of weeds
to fret about what it has a right to.

Wally Tells Beaver About Sex

Wally has a crewcut.
Beaver does not. Wally knows about sex.
Beaver does not. *Here's how*
you do it. The boys are in the kitchen.
Wally takes a giant pickle
and crams it halfway into a milk bottle.

Jeez, Wally. How are you going to get it out?
It gives up with a *thwop,*
like the sound a plunger makes
pulled back so fast
its rubber skirt turns inside out.
Dad does that?
Sure, Wally says. *He had to.*
At least twice.
Once for me.
Once for you.

Wally hangs out with Lumpy.
Beav sits halfway in the tire swing all afternoon,
his butt hanging out the back.
He doesn't say anything
to his mother when she unpacks the groceries,
to his father when he arrives home with a briefcase of papers
that Beav tried to read once but ended up
turning into jet airplanes,
much to Wally's delight and Ward's dismay.
Now Beav sings to himself.
Maybe he'll grow up to be a singer.
It's the first time he's ever thought that.

He sings loud.
He sings soft.
He likes soft the best.

If You're Fifteen, So Much Is Expected of You

Do you want to?
the girl asks.
Sure, the boy says,
though he really doesn't know
what she wishes from him.
So he lets her take his hand
and press it to her bosom.
The boy has always loved that word.
Bosom.
What is he supposed to do now?
He does not let himself take too much pleasure.
He knows
what might come of that.

Ricardo? Ripley? Rasputin?

Rafe, I repeat to the doctor
who, each time he says the name,
says it wrong and with the smile
that I've grown used to from doctors
when I make the mistake of telling them the truth
about the boy I visit
by stepping through full-length mirrors.
I am already standing over my friend's dead body
old women have stripped of its royal garments
because, as everyone knows,
to get into heaven you must be as naked
as when you were born. Even the snakes
have climbed the winding stairs
to the prince's chamber,
as if anyone as handsome in death as he was in life
is worth the risks. They circle silently
because who better understands how to grieve
than those who know the earth
in a way no one with arms and legs can?
Before I can stop myself,
I am sobbing in the doctor's office
and he stares at me, realizing
he's got to do something but not knowing what.
I'm sorry, I cry, but I'm not talking
to the doctor. *I'm truly sorry.* The snakes
loop up my legs and around my waist
as if they know the only comfort possible
is one body pressed against another,
and now at last they sing.

No Excuse

The door opened
on its own
when I was eleven and found a room in the house
no one else knew about.
It was empty of everything but a table
and a book of matches.
I took off my clothes. I wanted to be as naked
as the flames. I insisted
they touch me everywhere. Fifty years later
I am still going through that door.
Yes, I know:
People need me, and I need them.
But I still go through that door
when I can.
I don't knock.
I am expected there.

3

1. Caesar thought that Crastinus would be an example
of courage for the rest.
2. We know that Caesar placed him in command of the first maniple.
3. Caesar tells us that Crastinus was killed while he was fighting bravely.
4. He had many men that, like Crastinus, trusted and obeyed him.

Exercise taken from B. L. Ullman: *Second Year Latin*
(New York: Macmillan, 1957)

The Infancy Gospel of Thomas

What are you doing? I ask Jesus,
though it's obvious, this time, He's playing
with water—that is, making it do His will.
He's invited a stream to divert itself
into little pools and then, with soft mud, fashioned
twelve sparrows.
     What are you doing?
Joseph grabs his son by the ear.
It's the Sabbath, boy!
But Jesus pulls away and claps His hands
and the sparrows take flight,
chattering all the way up to the sky.
     What are you doing?
I implore Jesus
when I find Him standing over a boy
who'd bumped into Him on purpose
the way some boys do
in order to say, *Get out of the way!*
without having to say *Get out of the way!*
     What hurt did the water do you?
I confront the sneering son of Annas
who, with a willow, has pummeled the water
Jesus had just befriended.
     Then shall you be withered like a tree
that bears no fruit or leaf.
That's Jesus talking just before
he blinds everyone in the crowd
that, like a fist, has closed around him.
     Enough, I say
and lead Jesus away before He has a chance
to do one more thing He'll regret.
You can never tell with Jesus.
One minute He's sending a father to hell.
One minute He's saving his son.
     What are you doing? I ask
as Jesus undoes my tunic.
What are you doing?
Nothing, Jesus says. *Nothing at all.*

Ricky Nelson Inquires about Fellatio

Ricky knows not to ask his father
or his mother. Ozzie's always home.
No one knows what Ozzie does
for a living, except get in Harriet's way.

David is Ricky's only hope.
But David's locked inside his room
though Ricky keeps knocking.
Just today a man their parents' age stopped his car—

a Mercury— Ricky's crazy about Mercuries—
and opened the door so slowly
Ricky wasn't prepared for the surprise:
the man wore nothing but a watch

and wingtips so polished
Ricky noticed the watch reflected in the man's right shoe:
a Bulova. Next to expensive cars
Ricky loves expensive watches, especially ones so heavy

it's almost hard to lift your hand.
That's why Ricky's pounding on David's door
right now. David's been studying First Year Latin
and so maybe he knows

what the word means.
Ricky likes how it has so many vowels.
What did you say to the man? David asks.
No thank you.

Not today, thank you,
the way his mother talked to door-to-door salesmen.
David pretends he knows so much
but really has to look up everything:

Fellatio: subservient act of orally stimulating....
Ricky and David look up *subservient,*
though they could've asked their mother that.
Or their father, for that matter.

What Not to Tell the Girl You're Dating

If you want to get lucky,
don't talk about your imaginary friend
or the intrepid sister you made up
for this friend. Girls say they want to know everything
but aren't really interested
in how, at six, maybe eleven—okay, even fifteen—
you'd come home and close your door
and let yourself be seized by men
who wanted to do more
than capture you. Don't show your date
the wrists which never quite healed.
Don't talk about how delicious it felt
to have your hands free again.
What girl wants to make out
with a boy who, instead of nibbling on her ear,
babbles about his imaginary friend's
kid sister, her dark eyes,
how she cut away the cords that bound you?
Who in this world wants to hear your adventures
in that world? The one that exists
only because you say it does, a land so foreign
it can be found on no map,
its vocabulary different from what you use on the phone
or in the classroom or after football.
Did you really hope to carry back a little
of its language, its exotic and watery vowels,
ancient, honorable consonants?

Gestures Invented by Sixteen-Year-Old Forced to Read Quintilian

Plan to use one gesture for every three words.
Do not anticipate words with gestures, nor allow words
to out-pace their gestures. For example, to state a fact
make a circle with thumb and forefinger, extending
the remaining three fingers. Or to express horror,
turn both palms to the left.

—Quintilian: *Instituto Oratoria*

1. For when too tired to do a job that must be done: The fingers of both hands at attention like soldiers.

2. For when you don't wish to face what you know you must face: The first two fingers of each hand hard against the eyebrows as if to drill the truth home.

3. For when you want something you know you can't have: The tips of the first two fingers of each hand making circles in the temples, consoling even the bones of the skull.

4. For when you know something you don't wish to know: The hands covering the eyes, the fingers splayed.

5. For the inevitable moment when the lights are turned out and you can't help thinking that you're going to die some day and there's nothing you can do about it: One finger rubbing up and down the bridge of the nose.

6. For when surprised by a thought so profound it seems unlikely you thought it: The left hand flat on the skull, fingers splayed.

7. For when afraid to be angry because you're not sure what you'll do: The fingers of the right hand lightly caressing the skin just before the ear.

8. For those familiar moments when the brain recommits itself to misery: Two fingers on the lips to keep the mouth from saying too much.

9. For those rare moments when you're sure you'll be punished for being too happy: Both hands, like parentheses, on either side of the skull.

10. For when you stop in the middle of what you're doing and wonder what is the point of doing it and then go back to doing it: The knuckles rapping the forehead.

11. For when you wake up and the birds are clamoring once again for your attention and the light's rushing into every room and even the cats know it's time to get up and you can't believe only a few hours ago you could think of nothing but the fact that someday you were going to die: The heel of the right hand to the forehead.

SPCA

At the SPCA, the boy inquired,
Which one is going to be gassed
first?
The girl who unlocked the cage—
working off her community service,
she said, though he hadn't asked—
pointed to fur
in the corner.
It looked like a hairball.
The cat must not have known
it was due to die.
It did nothing to win anyone's affections
but bristled
and turned its back to the door.
The boy thought he could hear it
grumbling.
Apparently they'd disturbed it
at an inopportune time.
Do cats dream? the boy wanted to know.
I don't even like cats,
the girl said. *I do,*
the boy said
as if it needed saying.
Much to his surprise,
the cat didn't scratch
or even hiss
when he picked her up.
Yes, it was a she. He checked.
It seemed important
to know,
though that changed nothing.
Of course he renamed the cat
Schrödinger.
What else would a solipsist call his cat?
The cat let his fingers question
her chin, the little pockets of soft and hard
just below each ear.

His right hand introduced itself
to her spine, fur the color of a river
after a long rain.
Are you sure you want this one?
the girl asked
as if she couldn't comprehend
anyone, much less a boy her age,
wanting anything
no one else wanted.
The cat was clearly not grateful
to be carried out of the SPCA.
But the boy hadn't come looking
for gratitude.

Tercio de Muerte

Every morning, I step into oncoming traffic,
flashing my coat like a matador's cape,

and stare down El Dorados and Wranglers.
At my age there aren't many advantages

to being skinny, but it's what keeps me alive
in the middle of Memorial Drive:

cars rush by so close
I almost run my hand over an Impala's shiny coat

or leap into an open Mustang convertible
and, for a moment, I'm not a kid with a lisp

but a bullfighter staring down Taurus
and Imperial, Lincoln and Cadillac.

It's a miracle no one calls the principal to complain:
not the Dodge Caravan full of preschoolers

nor the Jaguar, late for a meeting,
that can't afford to kill a kid with a mouth of metal.

Here's one of life's few pleasures:
to be at the center of so much

speed, so many atoms
going one direction and you another,

and you, tempting the world to run over you,
know it wouldn't dare.

Salome Scolds Her Skeptical Hand.

As the Lord my God lives, if I do not insert my finger and examine
her condition, I will not believe the virgin has given birth....
Then Salome inserted her finger and cried out, "Woe to me for my sin
and faithlessness. For I have put the living God to the test and,
see, my hand is burning, falling away from me."

Protoevangelion 19:3-4

Hand, you're worse than the eyes.
You must see everything

for yourself.
It's not enough to listen to a bird;

you must cut open its throat
and fondle each note. If you could,

you'd drag a star out of the night
just to get your paws on it.

Broken glass tried to teach you,
unsheathed blade.

Must you make sure each wound hurts
as much as you thought it might?

Old narcissist, just because you suffer,
shall the rest of the body too?

Why Jesus Befriended Me

> *Also there was in him another marvel; when I sat at the*
> *table he would take me upon the breast and I held him;*
> *and sometimes his breast felt smooth to me and tender*
> *and sometimes hard as stone.... Another glory will I tell you,*
> *brethren. Sometimes when I would lay hold on him, I met*
> *with a material and solid body, and at other times again,*
> *when I felt him, the substance was immaterial,*
> *as if it had not existed at all....*
>
> Acts of John: 9:1-13

He liked to draw in the dust.
I liked to draw in the dust.

He liked to tickle. I was ticklish.
We both hated baths.

Even after playing with the pigs,
he smelled of rain and flowers.

The goats followed him everywhere
with their list of grievances.

The first time we met, he summoned snakes
out of me and sent them

to the desert to do whatever it is snakes do.
There was no end to the demons

coiled inside me.
At last he had a body to practice on.

He placed his fingertips lightly
on my eyelids and, just before I fell asleep,

I tasted death on his lips.
He kissed me as lightly as rain might.

The Secret

Lie down, the girl said.
     He had so many wounds
and she'd been searching for someone
     to heal.
But even completely undressed
     it was obvious
the boy was hiding something.
     Once a man tried
to pry the secret out of him
     and might've if the boy had
known what the secret was
     he clutched
close to his breast
     like a sealed document
someone had trusted him with
     even if
he couldn't be sure who
     or when
or what they'd wanted from him.
     He read everyone's face.
His friend's father?
     His brother's roommate?
A man on the subway?
     A woman in the shadows?
A teacher staring at him
     across a lecture hall?
On a library table, a book left open
     to a particular page?
A car slowing down,
     a window being rolled open?
Are you the one meant
     to break the seal?
Or are you?

My Life as a Patient

1

Are you seeing a doctor?
my professor asks, noticing the burn marks
on the wrists my cuffs tried to hide.
If only that were enough: to *see* a doctor.
To look at him for a while
and then close the door and drive off.

2

Visits! That's what my parents told me
to call my trips to the doctor.
As if I just happened to be in the neighborhood
and decided to pay a call
on a Harvard-educated man who spoke softly
whenever he talked about sex,
and he talked about sex often.

3

Finding me naked,
fire does not turn away. It needs me
as much as I need it.

4

If, when I was seven, you'd asked me
if my mother ever tried to kill me,
I'd have said no,
she wasn't really trying to murder me.
Just teach me a lesson.

5

That's ridiculous! the doctor laughs
when I admit I'm still burning myself.
By now I should've learned
to tell a psychiatrist only what's not
too difficult for him to hear.

6

I'm just visiting, the flame says
after I light the next match.
No, stay, I beg.
Stay as long as you can.

A Private Tutorial

Take off your clothes, he said as casually
as one might say, *Pull up a chair.*

Read, he said, as if that was the most natural thing
to do naked.

Start where I've marked the page.
Did you really think your teacher would be kinder

once you had your shirt off? He was, after all,
a scholar so famous even your parents knew of him

and he had courted you with metaphysical poets
and Camembert cheese on imported wafers.

You should've known you can't desire
and not suffer.

This man wasn't making love to you
but testing how much he could ask

of your body. You left as one might leave
any private lesson. You even shook

his offered hand and thanked him
the way you might express gratitude to the sea

for letting you go
after it had tried to drown you;

the way you thank the dark
for letting the light have you back.

No, I Tell Jesus Again

Don't. I pull away from Jesus
when He takes my hand again
and holds it to His breast, His shy, erect nipples
that could make anyone a true believer.
I shrink back the way a flame might.
Afterwards, when Jesus and I bathe in the river,
I don't mind the cold.
I let it penetrate me
everywhere. Jesus splashes me,
I splash Jesus,
and so we spend another day.
Another night:
putting off a journey
we cannot put off much longer.

The Other Disciple

Of course, you've not heard of me;
I was so good at chores,
no one noticed I was doing them.
You couldn't expect the apostles
to douse fires, the future St. Paul to empty his own chamber pot.

You try disposing of fish bones and bread crumbs
left by 5,000 hungry believers
or bathing all those healed lepers
or teaching a blind girl to read
after she's been given her eyesight back

or finding something to occupy a man
just emptied of demons—he who'd been Legion
now just an ordinary man
with no special purpose.
If you are on your way to Calvary,

you need someone like me
to rub your back, pick the bugs out of your beard,
lie down next to you the way a dog might,
your breathing timed to his.
If you're heading to Jerusalem

to die (that is, to provoke men into killing you),
a servant like me comes in handy.
I didn't want to watch the nails
hammered into Jesus, but I refused to
look away. I waited in the shadows

like a dog for his master
And, when I proved of no more use to him,
I left. That's what servants do.
They don't have to die just because their masters do.

4

Review: substantive clauses of result

1. *It happened that Pliny's eyes were very weak.*
2. *And so he writes that he studied in a dark bedroom with his ears.*
3. *Let the windows remain closed! The light hurts my eyes!*
4. *Although Pliny did not think that wine injured him,*
   nevertheless he used it very sparingly.
5. *The fact that my eyes are weak does not keep me from seeing*
   that my friend has sent me a very fat hen.

(Exercise from B. L. Ullman: *Second Year Latin*
(New York: Macmillan, 1957)

Crossing Jordan

We tie the blindfold loosely
over the eyes of the ninety-year-old woman
who uses the same kind of walking stick
mountaineers do. Softly
over the failing eyes of her elegantly coiffed neighbor
who spent her middle years in jail
for poisoning her husband. We blindfold the young man
just back from Iraq; the mother
of the boy studying ballet; the father
of the boy who wears a helmet to Sunday services.
Though no one came to church today
expecting to get their feet wet
or have their faith tested, we are all crossing Jordan
this morning, led by the six teenagers
whose parents still insist they come to church.
The kids' hands are surprisingly gentle
but firm with the retired colonel;
the psychiatric nurse; the lady who seems in charge
of everything in the parish; her friend
whose son died last month of an overdose;
the woman who's always a bar of notes ahead
of everyone in the offertory hymn;
the two well-dressed men
who told no one they were getting married
till they showed up, wearing rings
so big no one could miss them.
The teenagers have brought enough blindfolds
for everyone. *Trust us,* says the tenth-grader
who just got her learner's permit.
Trust us, says the ninth-grader
who's failing chemistry despite all her hours
of studying. *Trust us,*
says the eighth-grader who dreams of being a DJ
and spins platters alone in his room.
Trust us, says the kid who just mastered his back handspring.
Trust us, says his sister who's still not sure
why their father left them.
We are crossing the river today.

Samuel Ephesians

It's up to you not to lose him,
I say as I tuck Samuel Ephesians Hammonds
into my son's fist. Wharlest Jackson is safe
in mine. Each of us today bears a dead man's name.
So many black faces fill the sidewalks,
it's hard for the police
to decide whom first to yank out of the crowd.
My boy rides on my back
in one of those contraptions invented for fathers
who've sworn not to be like their fathers.
I even like it when he pulls my hair.
At least that keeps him busy
as we march toward the Governor's Mansion.
This is the world you must live in, Little Chris,
I repeat, but Little Christian is busy
talking to the floppy dog stuffed with cotton
he goes nowhere without. *No, puppy,*
Christian's scolding. *Puppy, no.*
Doggy Dog has misbehaved again
and so of course must be punished
and then forgiven. Then it's time
for us to lay down Wharlest and Samuel
next to Oneal Moore, Cpl. Roman Duckworth,
Lt. Colonel Lemuel Penn, and Rev. George Lee.
But not Samuel Ephesians Hammonds.
Nothing persuades my boy
to surrender the man he's held for ten city blocks
tight in his right hand. With his left
he reaches for one of the candles
we've lit despite the fact that it's still day
or maybe because it is day.
Sometimes, in the midst of light,
you need more light.
Christian's beside me now, in one fist, a name;
in his other, a flame.

What to Do After Being Chased by the Police Again?

Look up. Waaaaaaaaay up!
It's the Friendly Giant on Channel 65
setting out *a little chair for one of you,*
and a bigger chair for two more to curl up in.
Today FG has a tuba
and he makes the most interesting music with it.
My son and I start dancing
though just a few hours ago
the two of us had been hunting for streets
the tear gas hadn't found yet,
Christian bouncing on my back, me
with a *Free Bobby V.* sign in my one ink-stained hand,
leaflets in my other.
But now Friendly Giant and the jazz cats
and my son and I tilt
and sway, prance and swivel.
There's terror and cruelty,
and then there's television
and dancing.
There's this moment
and then the next.

Today the Sunday Youth Group Burns the Wednesday Evening Prayer Session's Note

Don't play with the candles
was all it said. Don't the church ladies know by now
they're asking for trouble
leaving a lighter anywhere in a room
frequented by thirteen-year-old boys?
You try to stop a seventh grader
from playing with fire.
Almost as soon as Tyler sees the note
the room smells of burning paper,
then singed potato chips,
scorched goldfish; teenagers can't study the Bible
and not snack on something!
Today we're reading one of those troublesome parts
where Jesus, hungry for figs,
won't forgive the fig tree for not being fruitful,
and we're all a little irritated with Him
again. So Tyler starts twisting small sprigs
off the potted evergreen
we are turning into a Tree of Hope.
Here at last is something readily combustible.
Tyler gets us all busy setting fire to the needles,
and soon the room's fragrant with sulfur
and fir and we have to get some fresh air.
That's how Sunday school ends for us
some weeks. Smoke
and flung-open windows.
We all serve God in our own ways.

Close Your Eyes, I Tell the Men

Close your eyes, I tell the men,
but of course they don't.

At first. In jail
it's safer to keep your eyes open

even when sleeping, especially sleeping.
Shut your eyes. Just for a little while!

Nick stares at me. He's got no other weapons
but his eyes now,

and he's not afraid to use them.
I stare back until even he gets tired.

The intake officer can seize your wallet, shoes,
your *Autobiography of Malcolm X,*

but not what's imploding inside your eyelids.
Your mother may have found drugs

more deserving of her attention
than you, your father may have tricked you

into believing he'd be back,
but you could close your eyes when you were seven

or seventeen and there would be sky. Constellations.
Suns you could name.

Keep your eyes closed. For a few minutes more.
Yes, I am talking to you.

I4 B18 N37 G56 O68

Bingo!
my mother cries out
because it's about time
she won
even though she hasn't once
looked at her cards.
At ninety-five,
why bother remembering
all those permutations?
Bingo! Bingo!
she pipes up like a little bird
reminding the world
it's still here.
Luckily, I've jotted down enough
pairs of letters and numbers
to win us yet another
toucan. My mother has a room full
of pandas and pachyderms,
sea turtles, plush flamingos,
Beanie Baby panthers and king snakes.
Look what I've won!
For you! she beams
How do you do it, Kit? the nurses coo.
My mother's no fool. She knows
we're all in on the joke together.
Not a bad haul for a Wednesday,
my mother winks. We both look out the window
we looked out yesterday
and the day before.
Something new always in it: a leaf
the wind's just seduced
off the branch. Or a newspaper hustling by
carrying Vladimir Putin, Lady Gaga, and the Chicago Cubs
somewhere they hadn't thought to go.
Or a bird
too undistinguished
in its browns for us to worry

about naming it, though my mother
swears it's the same one
we saw two days ago. *Yes,*
I say. *I believe you're right, mother.*
It certainly looks like the same bird.
Yes, my mother says,
I thought so.

On Reflection

After I learned my friend's cancer had migrated
to his brain, I began to have trouble
with doors. I'd forget which way they opened,
my hand would slip
off their knobs, and I shied from windows,
doubting their sincerity.
Knowing he only had weeks left,
Herb kept a notepad by his hospital bed
and woke, every morning, ready to publish his dreams
to the whole ward. Under each finished poem
he'd write *On Reflection* and commence,
with the last words, working back
to their beginning, expanding each line,
and then reading it all aloud
as if he'd come to the cancer ward
just for a captive audience:
the attendants emptying his bedpans;
the oncologist he made to sit through his latest sestina;
the psychiatrist that Herb wouldn't allow to leave
till she'd attempted a ghazal.
When Herb grew too weak to hold a pen,
I copied down the few similes he still had strength for.
Then finally he could do nothing
but sleep, one eye open, one hand twitching,
reaching for something it had let slip.
Kleenex? Fountain pen? The poem
he'd grown too tired to finish?
Committed as he is to sleep these days,
his tired fingers keep busy on their own
with tissues or the edge of a sheet
as if they sense they've only so much time left
and don't want to waste it doing nothing.
Is Herb's mind still as greedy as ever,
one eye closed to look deep
inside, one eye open to let the light find its way back
to the brain? Today I steer clear of windows.
If my friend can't look out them,

I don't want to either. No door
is worth opening if Herb's not behind it.
Cancer, that fierce barbarian,
has set up camp in a man's glorious brain.
May every cell in its army
recognize the valiant kingdom they've conquered.

Light, Old Pedophile, You're At It Again

Light, you ought to be on a list
of repeat offenders.

It's your fault
I pull off to the side of the road

to watch bare-chested kids shoot hoops.
I've never outgrown longing

that'd be understandable in a boy
but in a man of years seems an aberration,

if not an abomination.
As a child I'd stay outside

till the dusk seeped into my bones
as if expected there.

I'd feel myself age
so much I stooped over

from the coming night weighing down my back,
the burden I'd carry upstairs.

I'd pull down the blinds and let the dark teach me
as much as it could.

In the light this is *this* and that
is *that*, but in the disheveled shadows nothing's

quite the same
and nothing's all that different.

*What if you had to live all your days
in the dark?* asks the light.

Choose one or the other, demands the light.
Choose both, says the dark.

When It's Time to Leave

Just before we flee, we burn our houses.
One by one, we open the doors
and let the fire have everything we cannot carry
on our backs: our arms with room
for only so many dolls and dresses,
books and kitchen utensils, blankets and drums.
We must even leave behind the sounds
heard every day of our lives: the morning birds'
bickerings; curtains reminding windows
of their narrow views; winds' ill-tempered
naggings; a furnace's absent-mindedness;
a roof's faithful recording
of every acorn that bruises it; trees
and the stories their branches insist on telling
over and over; even the secrets
the beds have kept till now.
No one can bring their dead with them,
so we scorch the burial fields, the battlefields;
not even a single well remains
for our daughters to come back to
so they might dip a bucket down
and draw up the very water
that once quenched their grandmothers' parched lips—
water their mothers washed babies in,
water they had gazed into and seen themselves,
all shimmer and ripple.
The village is set aflame
and, along with it, every reason to return.
How can you make a new life
if you're always longing for the old?
Here, we say to each child,
is a torch. Everything must burn.

5

O mind, don't hope for forgiveness at this late date.

S. Gaddons

Absolution? You?

You've just had two good days
of giving your hands permission
to enjoy themselves: lifting cups and saucers

out of lemon-scented suds,
helping screws find their new homes
in the shelves you built

for your grandson's expanding collection of mostly naked,
wildly muscled men shrunk
so they could fit in a boy's hands

and he could have them wrestle to their deaths
and then revive them.
You even made sure

to be on good terms with the cats again
after yesterday opening the one kind of tuna
they happened to despise

this week. The dog finally peed for you
outside, and for once your granddaughter agreed
to the wisdom of washing her face

before her mother got home.
And when you head to your own house,
you even let the sun persuade your face

it's safe to smile.
So why, when everything's going so well,
do you put aside your book

in which the count is making the best of his exile
at the Hotel Metropol—he's even adopted a child
and she's teaching herself Chopin—

and go to the door when you knew who's knocking.
And what has he come to tell you,
this familiar stranger?

You've had two good days.
That's more than you ought to be allowed.
He knows it. You know it.

Making Love in a House with Thin Walls

No, oh no, you groan
as if you hadn't expected your aging body

to surprise you again like this. *No, please, no*
almost as if you didn't want to be touched

so ruthlessly by pleasure, that exquisite pain
for which nipples, belly, groin yearn. *No!*

Please, no,
as if you aren't just making love

but being lowered off a cross.
Not *Yes,* that cry of triumph,

the mouth taking a man-size bite out of the air.
Not *Yes* like Triton rising from the sea,

whooping and hollering, braying
the way gods do. They don't cling

to the beloved the way someone might to a capsized boat.
No, no, no, no!

What a person rescued from drowning shouts
as if, wriggling on the sand, he's not yet brave enough

to believe he's been saved. *No:*
that nihilist

consonant, the vowel
gasping for breath.

Stepping Out of the Box

> This six-inch chapter is the stoneless grave
> of Bulkington. Let me say only that it fared with him
> as with the storm-tossed ship.

Please, I beg the class,
and they stare at me as they might at any old man
with a mob of hair and mustard stains
on a sweater that might've barely passed for stylish
thirty years ago. Please,
I say to the girl who just laughs

when I beg for her homework.
Please, I implore the boy who's made it a matter of principle
not to smile all semester. By now
I'm almost on my knees.
Can you blame my students
for being put off by anyone this desperate

for them to succeed?
Their prof's got that old-man odor no one wants
to be close to. What teenager likes to be reminded
of how he'll end up? Please,
I croon to the girl who leans back
in her chair with the nonchalance of a raindrop

on the petal reserved for it.
Please, I turn to the blonde kid next to her
who shows up every day
dressed so lightly he's only a few buttons away
from being completely undressed.
Okay, I've never wanted to have sex

with my students, but I wouldn't mind
getting naked with a few of them:
the girl who doesn't write but stabs her words
onto the page, every verb an open blade,
every adjective lethal;
or the boy who reads his poems

as if he can't believe the stunning possibilities
even a preposition can promise.
Instead of asking the roomful of young men and women to strip,
I read them a little Melville:
Consider the intrepid soul's effort
to keep the open independence of her sea.

And the kid who at the beginning of every class
stands in the doorway
as if still not sure she's in the right room
raises her hand no higher than her shoulder:
Will this be on the test?
No matter how many times I permanent-marker a square

on the wall and draw a person
of indefinite gender climbing out of the box,
it's still a cliché. *You're a cliché,*
a boy says, looking at me sternly
as if I'd just taken his hand and encouraged him
to dive off a cliff

instead of inviting him to leave the room
another way than he came in.
I'm already at the windowsill.
Please, I whisper to all my students. *Join me.*
I've pried open the window. I'm already halfway out.
The classroom's on the first floor,
but for some kids it's still far too dangerous.

Giant Battle Pack of Knights

Sixty knights, half grey, half black, jumble together
with no alternative but to go on fighting,

one on top of the other.
Put an axe in one man's fist

and he's got no choice but to cut off another's head.
What else can you do with a mace

but bring it down on the foe cowering before you?
The grey warriors bludgeon the black,

the black eviscerate the grey.
Fall in love with the bearded black knight

with the impossibly skinny legs
and you fall in love with the bearded, skinny grey knight.

Both have that look in their eyes
you'd expect in a man

preparing to kill another man.
You still have all those flails and poleaxes, gisarmes

and halberds in your desk drawer.
The knights are still fighting the same battle

they did when you were a boy,
still willing to sacrifice everything for a cause—

though you never were quite sure what cause it was
they'd decided to give their lives for,

just that they must do it
honorably. Over and over.

Cleaning House

1

Eleanor of Aquitaine, Mademoiselle de Sombred.
Clothilde Supert—today
I am getting rid of all my mother's roses,
all those Lady Hillingtons and Lady Banks
I've inherited, decades-old
magazines fragrant with Larkspur, Peruvian Lily,
California Pepperberry, Monkshood,
whole closets devoted to Dahlias, Orchids, Mignonette,
Sweet Pea, so many roses
I get a sneezing attack just turning the pages,
Mme. Plantier, Marchesa Bocella, Old Blush,
the Shepherdess, the Dark Lady, Mutability,
high-class courtesans strutting their stuff
in seed catalogues as obscenely glossy
as any porn magazine. I may do my good deed
for the day and donate them to the 4-H or the Boy Scouts.
Farewell, Duchess du Garmount,
Painted Tongue, Blazing Star.
May you win someone a merit badge.

2

When you hit seventy, it's time
for a reasonable man to divest himself
of magazines titled
Bound and Gagged, Blue Boy, Mandate, Honcho,
Black Inches, Celebrity Skin, vintage
porn I'm not sure where to discard.
The Knights of Columbus paper drive?
The dumpster behind K-Mart?
I drive around with my trunk full of nipples
and penises. What does one say
to those one loves?
Sorry, one world was never enough?
I feel a little guilty disposing of so many
barely legal youngsters: Spike leaning against a locker
holding his genitals the way a kid might

a special toy brought for show and tell;
Alicia wearing nothing but a whistle;
Sylvie so combustible
she looks as if she might set herself ablaze;
Stefan opening his mouth wide
as if the world's so tasty
he's going to swallow everything in it.

3

Windless Orchard, Cutthroat River, Xanadu,
Happiness Holding Tank, White Fungus.
I open magazine after magazine,
and there I am naked
in poses I struck decades before.
What will my children do with all these little mags
foolish enough to print poems
in which, years ago, I made a point of undressing.
Dead Angel, Cactus Flower, Sensitive Skin,
Hyacinths and Biscuits, The River Styx.
My grandkids don't need sestinas
titled "My Father's Cuticles," "Tongues and Slugs,"
"The Dropped Stapler Just Misses the Baby's Head,"
"Changing My Mother's Diapers."
Was there nothing I wouldn't write about,
nothing I wouldn't publish to the world?

Wind

It's one of those days the wind punishes the trees
for being trees. Pummels roofs, cars;
shatters skylights, windshields.
Reminds us how little we matter.
Makes us pay for thinking we could keep anything
from its grasp. Even the little dog Pixie
is like tumbleweed outside.
A girl stays home and sits at the window
and watches the storm ruin the flowerbed
her father planted in strict rows
before deciding not to live in this house
anymore. The storm doesn't care
about the bird feeder either,
the one the girl and her father made watertight
in the basement where the father has left the tools
that apparently he doesn't need
in his new house. The wind's busy this afternoon
toppling lawn chairs, picnic table, and the fiberglass castle
from which this girl used to rule
what, at five, she thought was the world
but really was only a few kids young enough
for her to boss. And the wrens?
You'd think they'd be the first to be blown away,
the convivial chickadees,
the rascal bluejays, the pert robin
who just last week posed on the forsythia's top branch
as if it were only right
we should paint his portrait.
The storm's rushing through the yard
searching for anything foolish enough
to be outside on a day like this.
The girl holds her dog close to her.
The dog's still trembling.
The rains charge down
to help the wind do what it can't do alone:
turn day into night so dark you couldn't see
a bird if there were one out there. You even doubt
anything that ephemeral ever existed,
anything that wedded to song.

You Have a Knife Stuck in Your Heart

You have a knife stuck in your heart
and so you skype your son
who, years ago, moved as far away from you as he could.
Look, you say.
There's a knife stuck in my heart.
And your son says, *Sorry, I see no knife.*

Someone has shot an arrow into your right eye.
He didn't mean to,
but that's no comfort to your eye.
Your boss apologizes.
Sorry, you can't have the rest of the day off.

A disease has rotted your face.
You take pictures to send to your brother,
but he has his own problems.
Listen, he says when you call him.
At least you still have a face.

You stare at the water glass
In your hand. *For godsakes!*
shouts your therapist,
handing you another pill. *Swallow!*

Don't fret, your wife whispers,
kissing the one side of your face that's not contagious,
sliding the arrow from your eye,
emptying the poison into the sink.
But, no, she doesn't pull out the knife.
Who knows what would happen if she tried?

Marching Band

Opa, why do you still have toy soldiers?
my granddaughter scolds
in that voice she often uses
to make clear how much she disapproves of me
being anything but an old man
whose job it is to pick her up from school,
get her a snack, and deliver her to Brownies.
Miles away, an old friend is dying.
He and I used to bring our armies over to each other's house
and line them up
as if that's all life boiled down to: deciding who
to place next to whom—
piccolo and drum, tuba and French horn
and, best of all, the euphonium's clear baritone,
the astonishing partials
between bass clef and treble.
Even after we packed them up,
our musicians couldn't stop playing
even if they wanted to, their trumpets
and French horns molded to their mouths
as if this were the chief reason
one was brought into the world:
to stay one's ground,
to make one's music there.

Free Speech

God hates lesbians!
the bearded man with *Jesus Is Coming* embroidered
on his jacket bellows at the pigtailed coed
in combat boots. Late for Chemistry,
she has more pressing things to worry about
than burning in Hell.
Does your daughter know you're a whore?
the man points to a harried young mother
with a calculus book in one hand and a three-year-old
in her other. *I bet you were buggered as a child
and now you like getting it in the ass,*
the pastor shouts at a young man
so Old Testament beautiful
he could pass for an angel.
What's it like having a Christ-killer for a teacher?
Pastor Aden asks a girl
whose professor's come to draw away his students.
Pedophile, you're nothing but a pedophile!
It's the voice you expect a knife to use
breaking through skin.
Pastor Aden's wife grips a Bible in her right hand
and a *Sinners Go Straight to Hell* sign in her left.
A preschooler hangs onto her overcoat's hem
and another child leans against her
while a third, in a camouflage jacket, stares past the crowd
as if trained to search the horizon
for incoming planes. The college students
start to enjoy shouting back,
You're the faggots! You're the fucking creeps!
Do you want to spoil my entertainment?
a young man scolds his Calculus teacher
who hadn't come to work today
expecting to be called a slut.
The pastor swirls the word in his cheeks
the way you might a big, juicy luggie
before you spit it out.

Look, this is way better than television,
a girl shouts at her Spanish teacher,
meaning better than trying to remember the difference
between *estoy* and *soy.*
Finally someone even more stupid
than she feels in *Recitación*
or College Algebra or Psych 101.
The students gather at the barricades,
preferring damnation
to midterms. Except for a girl who takes refuge
in a Student Union bathroom and stares at the toilet stall door
as if any moment someone might bash it in.
Except for a boy who leans against a tree
and tries to figure out why he can't stop sobbing.
Look up! Birds patrol the sky
like helicopters. And, even higher,
a hawk's so close to the clouds
any minute it could fly straight into heaven.

Lessons from the Acts of Thomas, Jesus's Twin

Don't offer Jesus lame excuses why you can't go where He's
  sending you.
You know you're going to be sent there anyway.

If you don't want to be put to work,
don't make the mistake of learning a trade.

If you catch Jesus whispering to an Indian king in need of a
  carpenter,
you can bet you're going to India.

If everyone in the foreign land to which you've been sold sits down
  to dine, sit down to dine. Taste everything.

If a flute girl gives you the eye,
give her the eye right back. She knows something you don't.

If a cupbearer calls you an ignorant fool, don't worry.
Eventually he'll be dragged through the streets.

Invited by King Gundaphorous to sing at his daughter's wedding,
politely refuse. Watch out

for any king, especially one named Gundaphorous.
Don't expect him to have a sense of humor.

When he leads you by the ear to the bridal chamber,
then sing.

Trust your twin to show up in time
to start trouble, as He often does. Jesus can't help it;

fornication's always on the tip of His tongue.
Be a little suspicious of the bridegroom's gratitude

for being spared the honeymoon.
Beware a king greedy for heirs. Fathers are rarely grateful

if you crash their daughters' lavish weddings
only to preach chastity,

even if you prove to be the Son of God
or His twin brother.

Don't hang around. Get out of town as quick as you can.
And take the flute girl with you.

Work to Do!

In my grandfather's *Book of Knowledge*,
you'll find men hard at work on every page:
a crew pouring roads to *introduce one coast to another*;
another equally industrious gang dropping cable
so *Queen Victoria's words might travel 2,300 miles*
over the bottom of the sea to President Taft;
foresters draining a tree of its sugar;
machines spitting out matches (*24 million a day, each's head*
dipped in enough sulfur to burn down a city).
Even the poems keep busy
delivering overland mail and defeating Turks,
and the birds have jobs too—
not just building nests, but preventing plagues.
According to the *Book of Knowledge*,
even sperm face *arduous and often unrewarded labors*.
Grandfather, look at me now, still working
late into the night, still bent
over my notebooks, still trying
to be faithful to *The Kings Who Made Prussia Great*,
The Men Who Broke the Romans' Power,
The Royal Fish in Glistening Armor,
The Boy Who Asked for More, *The Prince Who Was Poor*,
The March of a Broken-Hearted Army,
The Flowers in Jack Frost's Garden.
So much work yet to be done!

The Story of a Boy

The old man used to have a friend
who loved words so much
she thought everything was a good subject
for a poem. She didn't even get tired
of the old man's poems about boys
who pretend to be invisible
or think they are robots
or linger in public restrooms
or dare cops to beat them up
so they can have a reason to be full of rage.
That boy was not the boy
the old man had been, but close enough
and different enough for him to give the boy
the courage he never had.
Now the old man's friend is dead—
Dead? What a word to use
for a friend—what's the old man to do
a few years away
from being dead himself? And the boy?
What then will become of the boy?

Last Wishes

1
If I have to die—and
    who doesn't?—
  I'd like to die with a choir
next to my bed, boys whose voices
        haven't changed yet
  singing Mendelssohn's
On the Wings of the Dove on a cd
    I bought in one country's cathedral
  to listen to
in another's darkened room.
    Far away, far away I rove.
  In the wilderness build me a nest.
Those few last, brief, inflated words'
    foolhardy surrender
  to the lyric.

2
If I must go—and now it's getting less
    of a question of *if*
  and more of *how soon*—
I prefer to die taking a nap
    with an old cat
        on my chest, one just as tired
as I am. Let me lie down after breakfast
    and breathe my last
  listening
to cars approaching,
      as they often do,
  with the self-importance
of messengers. My final minutes
    devoted to the sounds
    of my wife pushing through
the newspaper's brambly thicket
    of plagues
    and wars,
her morning sighs over cereal
      and the sports page.
  I love how she takes her time

with each victory, each loss, her spoon
        finding the very last sweetness.

3
Okay, maybe no dying
        with my eyes closed.
        Instead, let me pass away
while studying a book
        I remember depending on,
        Victims of the Latest Dance Craze
or *Miss Plastique, River of Saris*
        or *Living in the Sky, Lift,*
        or *Pear, Lake, Sun,*
100 *Tifton,* or even *Paradise Lost;*
                my pencil
        in the middle of a discussion
with an impertinent verb
        or oohing and aahing
        over an unexpected adjective.
Let me stay busy till the end,
        filling the margins
    Milton kindly left
so I could talk with him
                long distance,
    my question marks
quarreling with his stalwart commas;
        I can bear dying
    better
if I do so while conversing
            with Geoffrey Chaucer
    or George Herbert,
Lisel Mueller or Lucille Clifton,
            my exclamation marks
        making sure Marie Kane,
Betsy Sholl, Audre Lorde, Ethel Rackin,
            and Vida Chu know
        how grateful I am
for the blank space
            they filled with words
        left—I am certain of it!—
just for me.

The Solipsist Prays the Only Way He Can

He places one stone
on top of the other.

The first, the Atlas stone, must be willing
to bear more of the world

than could possibly be demanded of anyone.
The next stone must resign itself

to being pressed down with medieval weight
that could make even an angel confess.

The third must accept what is asked of it.
For the fourth, pick one whose center slopes into a dry lake

ready for whatever requires a small hollow.
The next stone must be speckled—

with little pinpricks of light in it—
yet dark enough

for someone to imagine these are stars,
that it's possible to cradle the sky in one's hands

and place it carefully
on top of a slightly larger stone.

The sixth should be of the right size to accommodate
a slightly smaller stone.

The stones must always be in danger of toppling
but not piled so high

they tempt a kid on his way home from school
to make the cairn pay for being in his path

on a day when everything went wrong.
The penultimate stone shoulders a weighty responsibility.

It can't get away with being slipshod
or too steady. It's got to wobble

a little and put everything in jeopardy,
testing the hand that placed it there.

And the last? It must be a stone so smooth
the fingers do not want to let it go.

Someone you love is hurting and there's nothing you can do
to make the hurt less.

See, a man has said,
I am building a little tower for the gods.

See, a woman says, *my hands took their time.*
I've been as careful as I could.

I have done the only thing I knew to do.
Doesn't that count for something?

Acknowledgments

This book would not have been possible without the generous eye of Lorraine Henrie Lins, the intrepid commitment to poetry of Diane Kistner, the wise counsel of Anne Tax and Jim Fillman, and the enduring friendship of Helen Lawton Wilson.

Thanks to the ongoing inspiration of my grandchildren, Jake, Zack, Josie, Tyler, Maggie, and Sadie, and the remarkable gift life gave me: my daughter Nora and my sons Christian and Justin.

Thanks to Bernadette McBride for the prefatory poem and all of her brave poetry.

Thanks to Andrea Scarpino and Ronald Riekki in whose collection *Undocumented: Great Lakes Poets Laureate on Social Justice* the poems "Confiscated Weapons" and "Close Your Eyes" appeared.

Thanks forever to Pam and to Herb and Sandy. You watch over all of us.

About FutureCycle Press

FutureCycle Press is dedicated to publishing lasting English-language poetry books, chapbooks, and anthologies in both print-on-demand and Kindle ebook formats. Founded in 2007 by long-time independent editor/publishers and partners Diane Kistner and Robert S. King, the press incorporated as a nonprofit in 2012. A number of our editors are distinguished poets and writers in their own right, and we have been actively involved in the small press movement going back to the early seventies.

The FutureCycle Poetry Book Prize and honorarium is awarded annually for the best full-length volume of poetry we publish in a calendar year. Introduced in 2013, our Good Works projects are anthologies devoted to issues of universal significance, with all proceeds donated to a related worthy cause. Our Selected Poems series highlights contemporary poets with a substantial body of work to their credit; with this series we strive to resurrect work that has had limited distribution and is now out of print.

We are dedicated to giving all of the authors we publish the care their work deserves, making our catalog of titles the most diverse and distinguished it can be, and paying forward any earnings to fund more great books.

We've learned a few things about independent publishing over the years. We've also evolved a unique, resilient publishing model that allows us to focus mainly on vetting and preserving for posterity poetry collections of exceptional quality without becoming overwhelmed with bookkeeping and mailing, fundraising activities, or taxing editorial and production "bubbles." To find out more, come see us at www.futurecycle.org.

The FutureCycle Poetry Book Prize

All full-length volumes of poetry published by FutureCycle Press in a given calendar year are considered for the annual FutureCycle Poetry Book Prize. This allows us to consider each submission on its own merits, outside of the context of a contest. Too, the judges see the finished book, which will have benefitted from the beautiful book design and strong editorial gloss we are famous for.

The book ranked the best in judging is announced as the prize-winner in the subsequent year. There is no fixed monetary award; instead, the winning poet receives an honorarium of 20% of the total net royalties from all poetry books and chapbooks the press sold online in the year the winning book was published. The winner is also accorded the honor of being on the panel of judges for the next year's competition; all judges receive copies of all con-tending books to keep for their personal library.

www.ingramcontent.com/pod-product-compliance
Lightning Source LLC
Chambersburg PA
CBHW072359090426
42741CB00012B/3086